To

Brian and Bruce
Randy and Diana

And

all the boys and girls
who like Bible stories

Published jointly by
REVIEW AND HERALD® PUBLISHING ASSOCIATION
Hagerstown, MD 21740
PACIFIC PRESS PUBLISHING ASSOCIATION
Boise, ID 83707

ISBN 978-0-8280-1016-0

Library of Congress Catalog Card No. 76-55834

PRINTED IN U.S.A.

My Bible Friends

Etta B. Degering/Book Three

Illustrated by William Dolwick, Manning de V. Lee, and Robert Berran

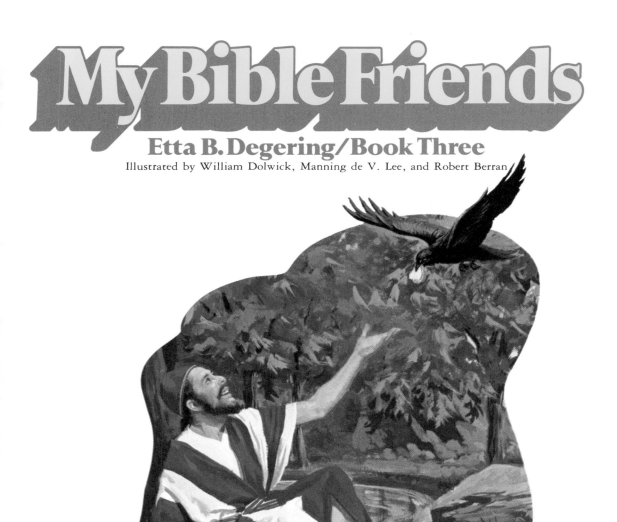

The stories in this book are—

Go Wash in the River

Elijah and the Time of No Rain

A Room and a Boy

Barley Loaves and Fishes

"Go Wash in the River"

(2 Kings 5)

Little Maid was far, far from home.
She worked for Captain and Lady Naaman.
She washed dishes. She ran errands.
Little Maid did everything
Captain and Lady Naaman asked her to do,
    except one thing.
One thing Little Maid did not do.

Captain and Lady Naaman prayed to an idol,
an ugly stone idol.
The idol couldn't see. It couldn't hear.
When Captain and Lady Naaman asked Little Maid
to pray with them to the idol,
Little Maid said, "Oh, no, I cannot pray to an idol.
I pray to the God in heaven.
He sees me. He hears me."

One morning when Little Maid
took Lady Naaman her breakfast,
Lady Naaman was crying.
"Why do you cry?" asked Little Maid.
"Captain Naaman is sick. He has leprosy spots.
The doctors cannot make him well."

"I know someone," said Little Maid, "who can make
    Captain Naaman well. If he will go
    to the prophet at my home, far, far away,
    the prophet will know what to do
    to make him well."
Lady Naaman told Captain Naaman
    what Little Maid said.

"I will go see the prophet," said Captain Naaman.
    "I will take him presents."
Captain Naaman rode in his best chariot.
He drove his fastest horses.
Men on horseback rode along behind the chariot.
At the turn of the road
    Captain Naaman waved good-by to Lady Naaman.
    He waved good-by to Little Maid.

The prophet saw Captain Naaman
and his men coming down the road.
He had heard about Captain Naaman's sickness.
He sent a man to meet him and tell him what to do.
"Tell Captain Naaman," said the prophet,
"to go wash in the river Jordan seven times,
and he will be well."

Captain Naaman said to his men,
    "Does the prophet think I am dirty?
    Does he think I need a bath?
    I will *not* wash in that muddy river."
Captain Naaman was angry, very angry,
    because the prophet told him
    to go wash in the river.
"I will go home," said Captain Naaman.

Captain Naaman started home.
The men on horseback rode up close beside him.
They said to him, "If the prophet had asked
     you to do some big thing,
     wouldn't you have done it?
     Why don't you do this little thing?
     Why don't you go wash in the river?"
Captain Naaman drove slower.
At last he turned off the road,
     and drove down toward the river.

The river was muddy,
    but Captain Naaman waded out into it.
He dipped down under the water.
Then he looked at his hands and his arms.
The leprosy spots were still there.

Captain Naaman dipped under the water again,
    but the leprosy spots were still there.
He dipped again. The spots were *still* there.
His men on the riverbank watched anxiously,
    as he dipped again, and again, and again.
But always the spots were there,
    and they were as large as ever.
Captain Naaman dipped under the water
    the seventh and last time,
    and the spots——

The spots were *GONE!*
Captain Naaman looked at his hands.
He looked at his legs.
He looked all over his body,
    but not a single spot could he find.
The spots were all gone. He was *WELL!*
His men clapped their hands and cheered.

Captain Naaman ran splashing out of the river.
He jumped into his chariot.
He galloped his horses back to the prophet's house
    to tell him thank you.
All of his men galloped along with him.

Captain Naaman bowed low before the prophet,
and thanked him.
He offered him the presents he had brought.
But the prophet said, "I cannot take the presents.
I did not make you well.
It was the God in heaven who made you well."

Captain Naaman and his men hurried home.
Lady Naaman and Little Maid
    were watching the road.
Captain Naaman waved to them. He drove faster.
When he came near he shouted,
    "I am well! I am well!"

And now when Captain and Lady Naaman prayed,
    they didn't pray to the idol
    that couldn't see and couldn't hear.
They prayed to the God in heaven,
    and Little Maid prayed with them.
"Thank You, God in heaven,"
    prayed Captain Naaman,
    "Thank You for making me well."

Elijah, and the Time of No-Rain

(1 Kings 17, 18)

King Ahab was a *wicked* king.

He set up idols of Baal, and altars of Baal,
   along the paths in the woods.

"Pray to Baal," he said to the people. "Baal sends
   the rain to make your fields and gardens grow."

King Ahab built a beautiful temple.

He placed the ugly idol of Baal in the temple.

"Pray to Baal," he said. "Baal sends the rain."

Prophet Elijah looked down from the mountains
where he lived in a little house built of stones.
He saw the temple of Baal. It made him weep.
God came near, and talked with Prophet Elijah.
"I will teach the king and the people
that it is I, the Lord, who sends the rain,
not the idol Baal. Go tell King Ahab," He said,
"that there will be neither dew nor rain until
the people of Israel turn away from idols."

Down the mountainside hurried Prophet Elijah.
Across the valley to the king's palace,
    past the king's soldiers. . . . Elijah
    did not stop until he stood before King Ahab.
"As the Lord God liveth," he told the king,
    "there shall be neither dew nor rain until
    the people of Israel turn away from idols."
Then Prophet Elijah quickly left the king's palace.
God whispered to him—
    "Hide yourself beside the Brook Cherith."

"Catch Elijah! Stop him!" shouted the king.
    "Don't let him get away!"
But Elijah was already gone.
The soldiers ran in all directions to find him.
They went to his mountain home,
    but Elijah was not there.
They hunted for him in the fields,
    but Elijah was not there.
Even King Ahab joined in the search,
    but no one could find Prophet Elijah.

Elijah hid beside the Brook Cherith.
He drank the clear, cool water of the brook.
Every morning, after the sun came up,
    and every evening, before the sun went down,
        God sent ravens to bring him food.
Many, many days Elijah lived beside Brook Cherith.
The wild creatures became his friends.

Because there was no rain, the grass turned brown,
   the leaves fell from the trees,
   and there was no grain to harvest.
Finally the Brook Cherith dried up,
   and there was no water for Elijah to drink.
But God did not forget him—God never forgets.
"Go to the city of Zerephath," He told Elijah.
   "I have commanded a widow who lives there
   to give you food and water."

The widow of Zerephath was searching for wood
near the city gate when Prophet Elijah came by.
Elijah asked her for a drink and some bread.
Said the widow, "I have only a handful of meal
and a little oil. I am gathering two sticks

to bake the last loaf of bread for me
and my boy; after that we must die."
"Fear not," said Elijah, "make me a little cake,
for God has said that the meal shall not lack,
nor the oil fail until the day He sends rain."

The widow baked a little cake for Prophet Elijah,
   and drew him a drink from the well;
   she gave him a room in the loft of her home.
And it happened as God had said. Every morning
   there was a handful of meal in her barrel,
   and a little oil in her cruse—
   enough for the day's loaf of bread—
   and God sent water in the well.
So, during the time of no-rain, the widow, the boy,
   and Elijah had bread to eat and water to drink.

Three years of no-rain went by.
Then one day God said to Prophet Elijah,
     "Go, show yourself unto King Ahab,
     and I will send rain upon the earth."
Back to the land of Israel went Prophet Elijah.
He met King Ahab on a path.
The king frowned at him.
     "Is it you, you troubler of Israel?"
"I have not troubled Israel," said Elijah. "You have,
     because you turned away from God. Gather
     all the people of Israel to me on Mount Carmel,"
     commanded Elijah, "and all the prophets of Baal."

King Ahab did as Prophet Elijah said—
    all the people of Israel, and
    all the prophets of Baal,
    gathered together on Mount Carmel.
This day Elijah would prove who was the *true* God.

"Let us build two altars," said Elijah,
    "one to the Lord, and one to Baal. Let us place
    wood on the altars, and an offering upon the wood.
    The God who answers by fire—HE IS GOD."
All the people answered, "It is well spoken."

The prophets of Baal built their altar.
They placed wood on the altar,
   and an offering upon the wood.
They prayed to Baal from morning until noon,

"O Baal, hear us. Hear us, O Baal."
There was no answer.
They cried louder and louder; they leaped and
    they jumped around the altar; they cut themselves.
Still there was no answer.

When it was evening, Elijah said to the people,
"Come near unto me." And they came near.
He built the altar of the Lord, and dug a ditch
around it. He placed wood on the altar, and
an offering upon the wood.

Then water was poured over the altar;
    it ran down and filled the ditch.
The people watched and waited.
Looking toward heaven, Elijah prayed:
    "O Lord God, let it be known this day
    that thou art God . . ."

Almost before Elijah could say *Amen,*
    fire flashed down from heaven like lightning.
It burned up the offering. It burned up the wood.
It even burned up the stones of the altar,
    and the water in the ditch.
All the people shouted—"THE LORD, HE IS GOD!
    THE LORD, HE IS GOD!"
God heard them, and was pleased. That night
    He sent a great rain to water the earth.

A Room and a Boy

(2 Kings 4)

The Woman of Shunem stood on the doorstep
  of her flat-roof, mud-brick home.
She shaded her eyes with her hand, and
  looked down the dusty road that led by her door.
"Prophet Elisha and his helper come this way,"
  she said to her husband, the Man of Shunem, who
  was sharpening his sickle under an olive tree.
"The prophet walks slowly, and leans hard on his staff.
  I'll invite him and his helper to stop by
  and have bread and drink with us."

Prophet Elisha thanked the Woman of Shunem
for the bread and the drink. When she
invited him to stay and rest awhile, he said,
"Nay, we must hurry on. The sun is low,
and we have far to go."
As she watched the tired men climb the hill,
she said to her husband—
"Let us build a room on the roof of our house
so that when the prophet comes this way,
we may invite him to stay the night."

Brick upon brick, with mortar between,
   the Man and the Woman of Shunem
   built a room on the roof of their house.
The bricks were made of mud, and dried in the sun.
Brick upon brick, with mortar between,
   until the walls were just the right height.
Then a flat roof they built over the room,
   and last of all, a stairway leading up to it.

In the new room the Woman of Shunem
   placed a bed and a stool,
   a table for the prophet's Bible,
   and a candlestick for him to read by.
Every day the Woman of Shunem watched
   to see if Prophet Elisha and his helper
   were coming along the dusty road.

Late one day the prophet and his helper came by.
The Woman of Shunem invited them in
   to have bread and to stay the night.
When the prophet saw the new room, he was
   pleased, very pleased. "What can we do
   to repay your kindness?" he asked.
   "Would you have us to speak to the king,
   or the captain of the army for you?"
"Nay, my lord," said the Woman of Shunem,
   "my husband and I do not want any pay."

But Prophet Elisha wished to do a kindness for
the Woman and the Man of Shunem
because of their kindness to him. . . .
What could it be?
"I have noticed," said his helper,
"that they have no son."
When the Woman of Shunem again stood at the door,
Prophet Elisha said, "We shall pray God,
and this time next year He will send
you and your husband a baby son."
The Woman of Shunem was pleased, very pleased.

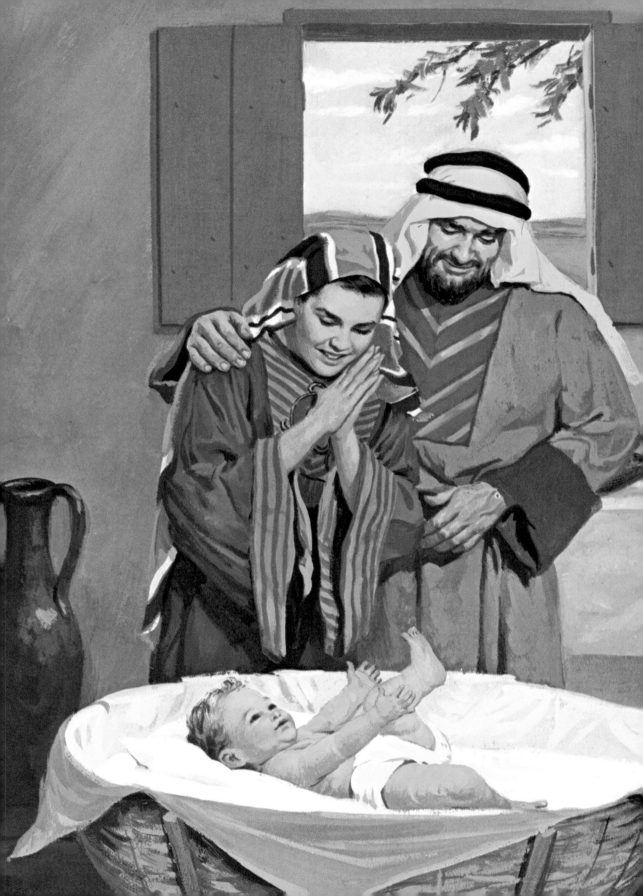

It happened just as Prophet Elisha had said—
    the next year a baby boy was born
    to the Woman and the Man of Shunem.
The baby's father and mother were sure that
    he was one of the finest and fairest babies
    in all the country round about Shunem.
And shouldn't he be?
    Wasn't he a prayed-for baby?

As the baby grew to be a boy, he and
    Prophet Elisha became good friends.
Now it was the boy who watched the dusty road
    to see if the prophet and his helper were coming.
"He's coming! Prophet Elisha is coming!"
    he would shout, and race down the road to meet him.
From there to the mud-brick house
    the prophet had double help in walking—
    his staff on one side and the boy on the other.

When the boy was as tall as a bundle of barley,
    he begged to go to the harvest field.
He couldn't cut grain with a sharp sickle, not yet,
    but he could pick up the grain that
    the reapers cut. And he did.
The sun shone hot, very hot, on his head.
Suddenly he dropped his armful of grain—
    "My head! My head!" he cried.
"Carry the boy to his mother,"
    said the Man of Shunem to a young helper.

All morning long the Woman of Shunem
    held the small boy on her lap,
    and sponged his head with cool water.
About noon she saw that he no longer breathed.
She carried him to the prophet's room
    and gently laid him on the prophet's bed.
Then she called to her husband,
    "Send me a young man and your fastest mule.
    I wish to ride to the prophet's house."

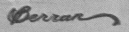

The Woman of Shunem saddled the donkey
while the young man saddled another.
"Ride fast," said the Woman of Shunem;
"ride as fast as you can."
They rode so fast that the donkeys
left a swirling cloud of gray dust behind them.
The Woman of Shunem rode straight
to the prophet's door, and told him
what had happened to the prayed-for boy.

Prophet Elisha went home with the Woman of Shunem.
He climbed the stairs to his room.
He opened the door, and there on the bed
　　lay his little friend—his eyes were closed,
　　his cheeks were pale, his hands were cold.
"Dear Lord," prayed Prophet Elisha, "show me
　　what to do, and make the boy live."

Berran

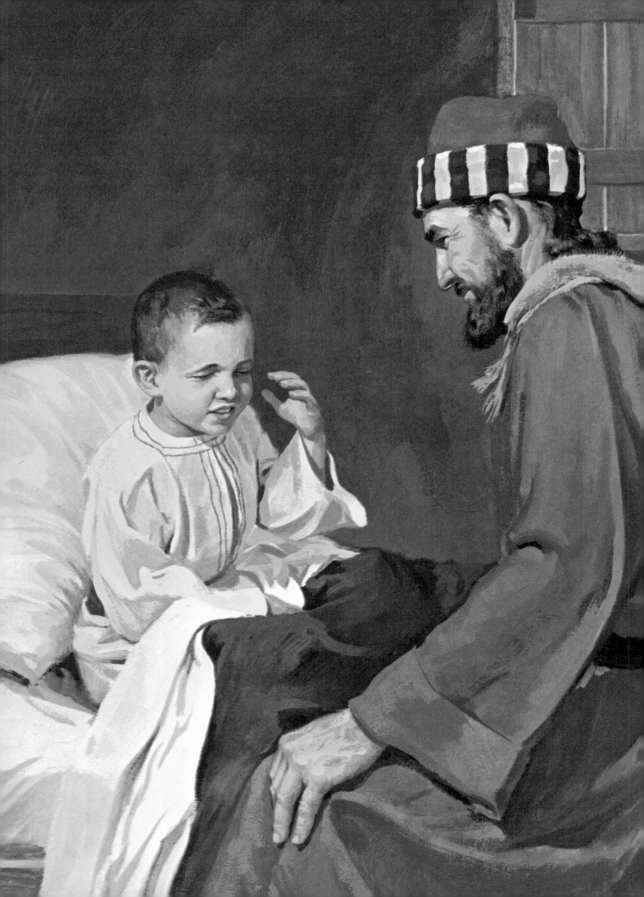

Prophet Elisha stretched his body
    over the little boy to warm him.
He put his hands on the boy's hands,
    his cheek against the boy's cheek;
    he breathed into his mouth.
Twice the prophet did this, and
    all of the time he was praying.
The little boy became warm.
    His cheeks turned pink.
He opened his eyes.
    He sneezed seven times.
When he saw his prophet friend he smiled.

Prophet Elisha sent for the boy's mother.
"Take up your son," he said. "He is well."
The Woman of Shunem knelt before the prophet.
    "How can I thank you?" she asked.
The prophet said, "It was God who made your
    boy well. Thank Him. Take up your son,
    and be happy." And she took him up.
Now, her son was not only a *prayed-for* boy,
    he was a *made-well* boy besides.

Berran

That evening we think we see the Woman of Shunem
    sitting on the doorstep of her mud-brick home,
    holding close her made-well boy.
The Man of Shunem joins them, and points
    to the room on the roof. "We thought
    to do a kindness when we built the room,
    but the kindness has come back to us, twice over."
"Kindness always comes back," says the Woman of Shunem.
"Kindness comes back," whispers the sleepy boy.

Barley Loaves and Fishes

(Matthew 14, John 6)

Little Lad lived by a lake—a deep blue lake—
  where at night his father went fishing.
In the morning Little Lad helped his father
  sort the fish he had caught.
They put the big fish in one pile,
  and the little fish in another pile—
  big fish, little fish,
  big fish, little fish.
Then Little Lad and his father went to breakfast.

For breakfast Little Lad had barley loaves.
Little Lad liked barley loaves.
They were round and crusty and good.
Barley loaves would make him grow strong,
    make him grow tall.
Then he, too, could go fishing on the lake.

One morning Little Lad saw many, many people
  going by his home along the lake shore.
They were going to find Jesus.
"May I go too?" he asked his mother.
"Why yes, you may go. I will make you a lunch.
  You will be hungry after that long walk."
Into a basket Little Lad's mother
    put five barley loaves
    and two small fishes.

She gave the basket to Little Lad
    to take with him on his long walk
    beside the lake.
Little Lad waved good-by to his mother.
Barefooted, he walked through the tickly grass,
    and the prickly weeds,
    and over the sun-warmed stones.
Little Lad was happy—
    happy to be walking along the lake shore
    on such a sunny morning—
    but most of all he was happy
    because he was going to see Jesus.

M. deV. Lee

Little Lad found Jesus on a grassy hillside
      talking to many, many people.
Jesus told such interesting stories.
He told about animals, and birds,
      and what it is like up in heaven.
Little Lad listened, and listened.
Sometimes he thought of eating his lunch,
      but always he waited
      for just one more story.

M. de V. Lee

"Little Lad, do you have any lunch?"
  asked a man named Andrew.
"Oh, yes sir, I have five barley loaves
  and two small fishes."
"Would you like to share your lunch
  with Jesus?" asked Andrew.
"Oh, yes sir, I would like
  to share my lunch with Jesus."

Little Lad gave his lunch basket to Andrew.
He watched Andrew take it to Jesus.
He saw the pleased look on Jesus' face.
And then he heard Jesus say to the people,
"Sit down on the grass, all of you.
We shall now have lunch."

Little Lad's eyes opened wide . . .
He thought, "There is not enough lunch
for all these people
in my little lunch basket."
He was about to go and tell Jesus
that there were only five barley loaves
and two small fishes in the basket,
but Jesus was asking the blessing.
Little Lad bowed his head.

Little Lad saw Jesus reach into the basket
and bring out barley loaves and fishes
for His helpers to pass to the people.
Little Lad moved closer to see better.
Andrew smiled and gave him a loaf and a fish.
Then Jesus reached into the basket again
and brought out more loaves and fishes.
Again, and again, and again,
Jesus put His hand into the basket
and always there were loaves and fishes.

"How can it be?" thought Little Lad.
   "In my basket there were only five loaves
   and two small fishes,
   but Jesus keeps taking out
   more, and more, and more."
And then he knew!
It was Jesus' *blessing* that made more—
   more barley loaves, more fishes.

When everyone had eaten, Jesus said,
   "Gather up the leftover food."
His helpers went here and there with baskets
   picking up all the small pieces.
Little Lad counted the baskets of leftovers.
   "1, 2, 3, 4, 5, 6, . . . *12 baskets!*"
What a surprise—and all from his little lunch.

Little Lad hurried home
to tell his father and his mother
how Jesus had fed a big crowd of people
from his basket of lunch.
And how when the people had eaten,
there was more left over
than he had to begin with.

M. deV. Lee

Dear Jesus,
   We thank Thee for our food today,
      Bless it to our good we pray.
   We thank Thee for Thy loving care,
      With others may we always share.
                                        Amen.